THE NEW FOREST

A GUIDE TO THE NEW FOREST HERITAGE AREA

CONTENTS

WELCOME TO THE NEW FOREST

**THE
NEW FOREST**

William the Conqueror may well have come as a visitor to this corner of England before he named it his 'New Forest' and claimed this land for his royal pleasure. In those days hunting had a practical purpose. As well as providing recreation and exercise for the court, the king's great retinue had to be fed. William strengthened the old Saxon forest law to conserve deer and wild boar but travellers were free to use the old Roman roads and forest tracks.

A welcome still awaits today's visitors. The forest law has been replaced by byelaws and the forest and country codes, which now seek to protect the forest's wildlife and traditions for future generations to enjoy. This guide gives you a fascinating insight into the history and ways of the New Forest. The natural story has pride of place. The ancient and ornamental woods have remained relatively untouched for hundreds of years.

The animal and plant communities within the woodlands and amongst the heather and moorland are rich and varied. The open forest, grazed by commoners' animals since Saxon times, has achieved with man's help an ecological balance, creating the landscape we so appreciate today. The greatest gift the forest can give to all who linger – whether visitor, resident, animal or bird – is peace and freedom from disturbance. With your help we will safeguard this special inheritance for future generations. I hope that you have an enjoyable and fulfilling time here.

MALDWIN DRUMMOND
Chairman of the New Forest Committee

The New Forest was created by King William I in 1079, just 13 years after the Battle of Hastings. This was the land of earlier Jutish settlers known as Ytene. For William, it was ideal for a new hunting ground, a poor, thinly populated district of furzey waste and ancient woodland covering over 200 square miles, yet close to his royal capital of Winchester.

In Norman times, the word 'forest' had dark overtones, signifying a land ruled without quarter by kings who jealously guarded their right to hunt unhindered by the petty concerns of local people.

To these poor folk, the forest law was brutal. They could not protect their crops with fences or hedges. They could not take timber for their houses. They could not catch game for their pots. The penalty was mutilation or death. But it was grudgingly conceded that they had to live on something, and to this end they were allowed to graze livestock on the forest wastes. This right survives 900 years later as animals owned by local people still roam across the forest. Their grazing has created and maintained the landscape that is such a well-loved part of our national heritage. Without constant browsing, the forest would soon disappear under heavy scrub and the wide open spaces would be no more.

The New Forest with its wonderfully rich collection of plants, birds and insects is now a national nature reserve. It is unique in this country for its sense of freedom. With the exception of the timber inclosures, no boundaries separate one habitat from another. Wild antiquity has determined this rich mosaic of ancient woodlands, windswept heaths, wet valley mires and fertile streamside lawns.

An intriguing paradox, this ancient forest, now managed by the Forestry Commission, changes but little each century yet is always alive and always on the move, forever advancing and decaying through a timeless ebb and flow of nature.

FOREST FACTS

New Forest Heritage Area:	143,550 acres (58,094 hectares)
Unenclosed common grazing land:	48, 854 acres (19,771 hectares)
Highest point:	Long Cross Plain 414 feet (125 metres)
Longest river:	Lymington River/Highland Water 15 miles (24 kilometres)
Largest pond:	Hatchet Pond, Beaulieu (created in 1792)
Tallest Tree:	Wellingtonia (giant sequoia), Rhinefield Drive. Planted 1852 Height 178 feet (55 metres)
Oldest Tree:	Common yew, Brockenhurst Church. Possibly 1,000 years old Circumference at 5-foot height: 20 feet (6.3 metres)
Average annual rainfall:	33 inches (800 millimetres)
Wettest month:	October
Driest month:	May
Average annual temperature:	10°C (50°F)
Visitor numbers:	Estimated visitor days spent in New Forest – 7.15 million

LEFT AND ABOVE:
The New Forest embroidery celebrates scenes of forest life. It was created by around 60 local people in 1979 to mark the 900th anniversary of the founding of the forest. It is on display in the New Forest Museum, Lyndhurst.

BELOW:
This plaque commemorates the planting of an oak tree in the New Forest by HM The Queen in 1979, depicted in the embroidery illustrated above.

People have lived in the New Forest for as long as they have anywhere in Britain, but visible evidence is hard to find. There are no prehistoric stone circles, no massive earthworks, no Roman villas or medieval fortifications, yet examples of all these can be found within a few miles of the forest boundary.

Although the region has always had some open land, originally there were far more trees. The vast areas of heather moorland now so characteristic of the New Forest were originally dense woods. These fell victim to Stone Age settlers who, using flints, teeth and bones, felled timber for building and cleared the ground for agriculture. The animals they brought with them were the first domestic breeds to graze the New Forest.

The change from woodland to heath accelerated with the bronze tools which appeared around 1000 BC and the Iron Age implements which followed.

Bronze Age round barrows are plentiful. These simple earth monuments, now capped in gorse, fern and pine, were the burial places of the early tribes. There are also a smaller number of defensive inclosure banks known locally as castles. These minor hilltop fortifications are thought to be the work of Iron Age defenders, and many date from the time of the Roman invasion.

Extensive field systems with worn down banks and ditches are certainly pre-Roman in origin and many from different times crisscross the forest. It was only the relatively recent introduction of wire fencing which allowed inclosures to be made without the necessity of earthworks.

The Romans, like all settlers to this district, knew the land was poor and unproductive. But they used the plentiful supply of raw materials (fuel wood, sand, clay and water) to found a thriving pottery industry. There are many known sites around the forest, each with a distinctive circular earth kiln and heap of pottery fragments nearby. New Forest pottery has been found at every Roman site in southern Britain. Coins found alongside the kilns suggest that the potteries were in production until the Romans left in about AD 410.

Following their departure, during the curious period of several centuries known as the Dark Ages, Saxons and Jutes from

HISTORIC MILESTONES

1079	New Forest created by William I.
1100	William II (Rufus) killed while hunting in the forest.
1483	New Forest Act allows inclosures for growing timber.
1611	First recorded felling for navy timber.
1776	Scots pine introduced at Ocknell and Bolderwood.
1851	Deer Removal Act – unsuccessful attempt to destroy all deer in the forest.
1877	Verderers' powers changed to protect commoners' interests (known as the Commoners' Charter).
1924	Forestry Commission takes over management of New Forest's Crown land.
1939–45	Ten airfields built in and around the forest including Beaulieu, Holmsley and Stoney Cross.
1949	New Forest Act – Verderers' Inclosures were created.
1971	New Forest declared a Site of Special Scientific Interest.
1992	Government agrees special status equivalent to a national park.

northern Europe invaded the New Forest. Although virtually nothing has survived from this period, their language has endured in almost all the local place names. The Domesday Book of 1086 gives us a remarkable picture of the New Forest in Saxon times, written as it was only seven years after the forest became a preserve for royal hunting. Throughout the Middle Ages, the forest was first and foremost a place not of trees but of deer, the supreme status symbol of the king's nobility.

It was not until the 14th century that the Crown's interest in deer conservation diminished as the demand for timber for naval shipbuilding and fortifications created a new importance for the royal forests. The self-renewing power of trees had been exploited for centuries to meet local fuel and building

RIGHT:
Ancient tumuli are found throughout the forest. They are just one example of many different types of historical sites and ancient earthworks.

BELOW:
Bucklers Hard village was created in the 17th century on the Beaulieu River. Many warships were built here using New Forest timber.

needs, but the new scale of timber production required for the Royal Navy prompted the inclosure of thousands of acres of forest land for timber growing, land taken at the expense of the commoners' rights to graze the open forest.

After 900 years, more than 100 square miles of the forest is still owned by the Crown. Since 1924 this has been administered by the Forestry Commission. Although the age-old suspicions between commoners and Crown have not entirely disappeared, problems today are largely settled by open discussion.

W A L K

At Canterton, a short distance from the village of Brook, a small three-sided cast-iron monument marks the spot where King William II (called Rufus after his red hair) is believed to have been killed. The inscription on the Rufus Stone reads:

Here stood the oak tree on which an arrow shot by Sir Walter Tyrrell at a stag glanced and struck King William II surnamed Rufus on the breast of which stroke he instantly died on the second day of August anno 1100. King William thus slain was laid on a cart belonging to one Purkess and drawn from hence to Winchester, and buried in the Cathedral Church of that City.

From this ancient memorial a pleasant 1½-mile (2.4 kilometres) walk begins by crossing the road to the car park and entering the woodland. This is a wet area of the forest at any time of the year, so be prepared for very muddy conditions underfoot.

BELOW:
A New Forest pony grazes peacefully in the shade of an ancient oak tree.

Map:

Brook

N

Lower Canterton

Pipers Copse

Upper Canterton

Sir Walter Tyrrell (PH)

Rufus Stone

A31

P

| 0 | Yards | 200 |
| 0 | Metres | 200 |

Canterton and the Rufus Stone: 1½-mile walk

For key to symbols, see map pp. 22-23

LEFT:
The Rufus Stone marks the spot where tradition holds that William Rufus was killed in AD 1100. The cast-iron pillar was placed over the original stone for protection.

RIGHT:
Fallow deer are by far the most common and easily seen species in the New Forest. Today's herds are directly descended from those animals first introduced by the Norman kings. This photograph shows a small herd of does beneath a dark November sky. For part of the year the bucks and does live apart in single-sex groups.

The woodland track leads downhill to a small stream. Cross the ford and take the track immediately to your left close to the stream bank. This will bring you out of the trees at Canterton Green. Make your way across to the small community of Lower Canterton. The road leads on to the village of Brook but you must turn left between the houses and follow the bridleway signposted at the junction. This path will take you back over the stream you crossed earlier and through woodland for a further 350 metres.

The lane continues for 800 metres to its junction with a road. Turn left (there is a postbox on this corner) and follow the road back to your starting point, passing the Sir Walter Tyrrell pub a few hundred metres before arriving back at the Rufus Stone.

BELOW:
The Sir Walter Tyrrell, a popular forest pub named after the knight who, it is said, killed the king with his arrow.

The free-roaming ponies form many people's image of the New Forest. They wander the open forest, kept in only by grids and boundary fences. What the visitor may not realize is that each animal grazing on the forest is owned by a commoner who to enjoy this right must pay a fee and have their pony marked with an individual brand.

There are six ancient Rights of Common (see panel on page 12), the most valuable and well-used being the Common of Pasture. Commoning is a way of life for many people, a tradition going back through generations. It survives here as a rare example of a rural economy that flourished throughout medieval England but has now been all

but lost elsewhere. Commoners are people who own land in and around the forest which has rights attached. About 350 of them exercise these privileges today and together on the open forest they run 1,800 cattle, a much smaller number of donkeys, pigs and sheep and over 3,000 ponies. Ponies are still part of rural currency although the demand today is more often for riding ponies than beasts of burden.

Only a small number of commoners are able to make a complete living from keeping stock. Most of them are part-time farmers supplementing their incomes from other work. Others simply keep one or two animals on the forest to maintain this age-old tradition.

The commoners' interests are represented by the Court of Verderers whose duty is to administer the commoning system. Every two months ten verderers sit in public at the Verderers' Hall in Lyndhurst to hear presentments* about the management of the forest. The court is a relic of the royal hunting forest and probably Britain's oldest court of law, originally established to manage the legal system that protected hunting for the Norman overlords. Today, as guardians of the forest scene, the verderers work in partnership with the Forestry Commission to balance grazing and the needs of commoners with the needs of conservation and heavy recreational use.

* A presentment is a statement or request made by any member of the public asking the verderers to investigate a forest issue.

The verderers employ five agisters, full-time officers who deal with the day-to-day problems that arise from grazing several thousand animals over 45,000 acres (18,000 hectares) of forest. The animals have right of way on the roads and the whole of the open forest now has a 40 mph speed limit to protect the ponies and cattle.

Each autumn, the agisters organize a series of round-ups, or drifts, where they ride the forest with commoners searching out and capturing ponies. Children ride alongside their elders, learning the tricks and skills gained from a lifetime's experience. Once caught, ponies are held in fenced corrals called forest pounds, where their condition can be checked before the onset of winter. Each pony is branded and the agister clips the tail to a special pattern once the grazing fee has been paid.

If the grazing of commoners' ponies and cattle ever came to an end, the open character of the forest heaths would soon disappear in a mass of scrub. Commoning is far more than a remnant of an ancient way of life – it is essential for the continued well-being of the New Forest.

ABOVE:
The verderers hold open court every two months. There are ten verderers, five elected by the commoners and five appointed by official bodies.

ABOVE LEFT:
Five agisters are employed by the verderers to look after the stock grazing on the forest.

RIGHT:
In the autumn, pigs are turned out onto the forest to eat the green acorns and beech mast which are poisonous to ponies. The pannage season lasts for at least 60 days.

The Stride family are practising New Forest commoners. Richard and Caroline have three boys who all expect to continue the commoning way of life when they grow up. When they were born Robert, Andrew and Philip were each given a New Forest mare by their grandparents to start their own herds.

The family run a herd of New Forest ponies and about 40 beef cows on the open forest. A few animals remain on the smallholding to provide milk, eggs and meat for daily needs. In the autumn their litter of pigs is 'turned out' during the pannage season when they feast on the free and usually abundant crop of acorns and beech mast.

Richard has worked for the Forestry Commission since leaving school. Having lived, worked and played here all his life he knows the forest as well as anyone. It was no surprise when he was elected a verderer by the commoners themselves. Caroline looks after the smallholding during the day but in the evening and at weekends it is a real family effort.

During late summer the annual drifts begin. Robert is old enough to help out and ride with the other commoners. Riding the ponies at speed requires great skill to avoid the many hazards of the open forest; accidents happen all too often.

There are many exciting moments in the forest year. The family look forward to buying new ponies or selling this year's foals at the Beaulieu Road pony sales. In the winter months, the point-to-points give the boys an opportunity to demonstrate their pony riding skills.

RIGHT:
Philip collects fresh eggs for the family's breakfast. His job is to look after the chickens on the holding.

RIGHTS OF COMMON

- *Common of Pasture* – the right to graze cattle, ponies, donkeys and occasionally sheep.

- *Common of Mast* – the right to turn pigs out on the forest during the pannage season, in autumn when acorns and beech mast have fallen.

- *Common of Fuelwood* – an allowance of burning wood for use in a dwelling (also known as Estovers).

- *Common of Sheep* – the right to depasture sheep.

- * *Common of Marl* – the right to take limey clay to spread on the commoner's land as a form of soil improver.

- * *Common of Turbary* – the right to cut turf for burning in a dwelling.

* The Rights of Common of Marl and Turbary are not currently exercised.

LEFT:
Ponies are sold at the Beaulieu Road sales. An important event for commoners, the sales are held five times a year.

RIGHT:
Riding a drift is an exciting but dangerous activity. The forest is full of hazards for the unwary, and children learn the ways of the forest from experienced commoners.

BELOW:
Robert with chestnut mare Tiger Lily and her foal Tigger.

RIGHT:
When not on the forest the pigs need to be fed daily.

BELOW LEFT:
Andrew and his father ride out to an autumn drift and a hard day's work.

BELOW RIGHT:
Not long ago every holding kept a milk cow for home needs. Caroline is milking Rosie, the family's Guernsey.

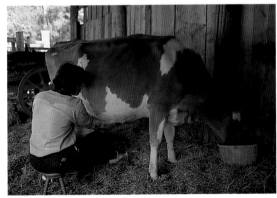

FRITHAM – A COMMONING WALK

This 2-mile (3.2 kilometres) walk takes you through Fritham, an unspoilt commoning community where many local people still exercise their ancient forest rights. The village retains a traditional pattern of smallholdings and farms, typical of communities all around the edge of the New Forest. The walk includes sections on country lanes without footpaths. Although traffic is usually light here, stay alert and whenever possible keep to the right to face oncoming traffic. Please keep your dogs under close control and preferably on a lead.

From Janesmoor Car Park, cross the road and follow the gravel track to the gate of North Bentley Inclosure. Do not go into the plantation but follow the fence along to your right until you reach the corner of the inclosure. Here, a wide wooded track leads you between the inclosure on your left and the boundary of Fritham's fields on your right.

Your way leads downhill, emerging after 800 metres onto a pleasant forest lawn crossed by a small stream. Beyond the bridge, follow the gravel track to your right up the hill towards Fritham, keeping the houses on your right. Continue along this lane, past an attractive little chapel, to the open area of forest lawn. To the left a pleasant 800-metre detour will take you down a lane to Eyeworth

Pond, while the main route takes you past the Royal Oak pub to the right. The much-loved Royal Oak has a long association with local commoners and foresters. Once called the Parliament of the New Forest, it remains a popular meeting place. The intimate back-parlour with its old wooden benches and blackened open fireplace is worth a visit.

RIGHT:
The Royal Oak pub at Fritham, once known as the Parliament of the New Forest.

FAR RIGHT:
In November the pannage season is well underway.

ABOVE:
Eyeworth Pond was created in the 19th century to provide power for a nearby gunpowder factory.

LEFT:
A 'forwarder' is used to bring round-wood from the forest and stack it at ride-side ready for the lorry to take it away.

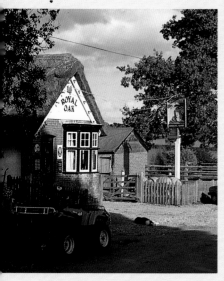

From the Royal Oak, follow the road down the hill between fields and small farms. The small animal pound at the bottom of the hill is used by local commoners to corral their animals at the end of a pony drift. In 400 metres, at a small triangular green, follow the lane to your right between high hedges for 800 metres back to Janesmoor Plain where your walk began.

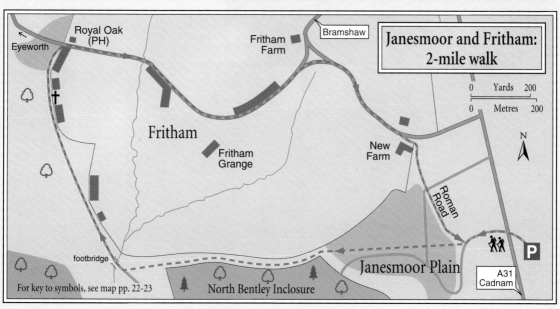

Janesmoor and Fritham: 2-mile walk

Eyeworth

Royal Oak (PH)

Fritham Farm

Bramshaw

Fritham

Fritham Grange

New Farm

Roman Road

Janesmoor Plain

footbridge

For key to symbols, see map pp. 22-23

North Bentley Inclosure

A31 Cadnam

P

N

0	Yards	200
0	Metres	200

THE FOREST AT WORK

The first enclosure of land for forestry dates back to a conservation measure taken as early as 1483. The New Forest had become an important source of timber for the navy and action was needed to make sure there was a constant supply of trees, especially as an oak tree the right size for shipbuilding could take 200 years to grow.

In 1808 the Crown started a 60-year planting programme in the forest. However, as ironclads replaced wooden-hulled ships, many trees that resulted were destined never to sail the seas. The fine oak woods still remain and while they yield valuable timber for building and furniture-making they are now more important for their wildlife and for the scenic contribution they make to the forest.

The 19th century also saw the arrival of new conifers such as douglas fir, corsican pine and norway spruce. These softwoods grew much faster than beech and oak, producing a crop of timber in 50 or 60 years as well as an income from the thinning-out which took place after 20 years until the final felling.

The Crown was keen to plant more of these conifers and as at that time it had the power of rolling inclosure it could inclose new areas. When existing woods were past

ABOVE:
Newly planted hardwoods such as oak have to be protected against browsing by deer. When small areas are planted, protective tubes are used as this is cheaper than deer-fencing.

RIGHT:
Each stack sold is marked with the name of the purchaser and the number of the contract.

the danger of damage by grazing animals they could be thrown open by removing the fence and new land enclosed. When people realized how much land was being taken there was a public outcry and Parliament was forced to intervene. A New Forest Act of 1877 fixed the maximum total area of enclosures at 18,000 acres (7,112 hectares). Of this only 16,000 acres (6,475 hectares) could be fenced at any one time.

The Act also recognized that parts of the forest were of great amenity value and designated them 'Ancient and Ornamental Woodlands'. These magnificent woods possess a medieval character, having been for centuries managed by woodmen and grazed by the commoners' animals. In contrast to the timber inclosures, the boundaries of these Ancient and Ornamental woods are difficult to define. They are not fixed by fencelines and are constantly changing. Clearings are created by the collapse of decaying giants or the strength of winter gales whilst new trees grow on the edges or in the tangle of dead wood lying on the ground. Today these pasture woodlands are managed by the Forestry Commission for their ecological importance and great beauty, not for profit.

It is important to remember that, for all its beauty, the New Forest is very much a working forest. Each year forest inclosures

LEFT:
Felling large trees is specialist work. Good training and safety precautions are essential. During the last 40 years forest work has become increasingly mechanized, the chainsaw replacing the woodman's axe and cross-cut saw.

RIGHT:
Powerful machinery is used to move heavy logs sometimes weighing 1 tonne or more.

BELOW:
Forestry workers relax and enjoy a summer meal break during a long day's work. More than 60 men work in the forest each day.

produce over 39,000 tonnes of timber, about eight large lorry loads each working day. Local industries use this for building, fencing and garden furniture. Some is sent away for paper pulp and chipboard.

Since 1924 the Forestry Commission has managed the forest and today employs over 100 people. Many other local people depend on the trees for their living including lorry drivers, sawmill workers, firewood merchants and traders.

A healthy working forest provides both income and employment. The foresters of today know they have to keep a balance between the needs of commoners' grazing, nature conservation and timber production, a challenge which they meet with enthusiasm and commitment. The fact that the magnificent woodlands of the New Forest are so productive yet still hold the power to capture our imagination is a testament to their success.

FORESTRY FACTS

Annual Production:

Conifers	35,000 cubic metres (tonnes)
Broadleaved	4,000 cubic metres (tonnes)

Main Products:

Saw logs	23,000 cubic metres (tonnes)
Pulpwood	10,000 cubic metres (tonnes)

Posts, rails, telephone posts and fuelwood:
6,000 cubic metres (tonnes)

Land Area

Open Forest	45,722 acres (18,512 hectares)
Inclosures	21,360 acres (8,648 hectares)

Total Crown land managed by Forestry Commission
67,082 acres (27,160 hectares)

WILVERLEY INCLOSURE – A FORESTRY WALK

LEFT:
A magnificent fallow buck in prime breeding condition prepares for the autumn rut.

BELOW:
A great spotted woodpecker returning to nest with a beakful of insects to feed its young.

This easy 1½-mile (2.4 kilometres) walk takes you on a circular route through Wilverley Inclosure, part of the working forest. Like all the plantations, it is enclosed by a fence to keep grazing animals from damaging young trees. Please make sure that you close gates behind you to keep animals out. Although the walk begins on firm level ground, part of the route takes you along grassy rides which can be muddy.

The route of your walk needs no detailed description as it is marked by blue-banded route posts. The 'Wilverley Stroll', at the beginning of the walk is a short circular route of only 500 metres on a level, firm surface suitable for pushchairs and wheelchairs.

On the Wilverley Walk you will see an attractive mix of conifers with traditional hardwood species, particularly oak, sweet chestnut and beech. Conifers have needles and are generally evergreen, whilst the hardwood trees have leaves which are shed each autumn. These hardwoods are normally called the broadleaves.

RIGHT:
Many inclosures were given fine cast-iron plaques in Victorian times.

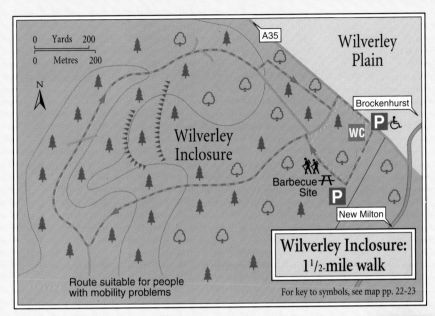

0 Yards 200

0 Metres 200

N

A35

Wilverley
Plain

Brockenhurst

P &

WC

Wilverley
Inclosure

Barbecue
Site

P

New Milton

**Wilverley Inclosure:
1½-mile walk**

Route suitable for people
with mobility problems

For key to symbols, see map pp. 22-23

BELOW:
The tubes seen here through sweet chestnut leaves protect young trees from the hungry mouths of deer, rabbits and other woodland mammals. They stay on for several years, also acting as small greenhouses to speed growth.

BELOW:
Permits are issued by the Forestry Commission to allow ponies and traps to use the forest roads within inclosures. In two locations (see pages 24–25) wagon rides through the forest are available to visitors.

Forestry is the science and art of managing woodland to provide a supply of timber and at the same time create a rich environment for wildlife and recreation. The variety of ages and species of trees provides a wonderful range of habitats. This means that the forester has constantly to balance the demands of timber production against the needs of the wildlife to maintain the well-being of the woods under his care.

The deer which are so delightful to encounter in the forest can cause great harm to young trees and, if left unchecked in numbers, would soon destroy whole plantations. Grey squirrels too are charming to see, but since their arrival here in 1940 have done untold damage by bark-stripping. In forestry terms they are regarded as a pest. Look out for many of the beeches that have suffered from their attentions!

Remarkably, this country still imports 90% of all the timber it needs. Each year Wilverley Inclosure produces around 1,000 tonnes of wood (about 50 large lorry loads). This is perhaps a small amount in the whole scale of things, but it is nevertheless a significant part of the New Forest's contribution to the local economy.

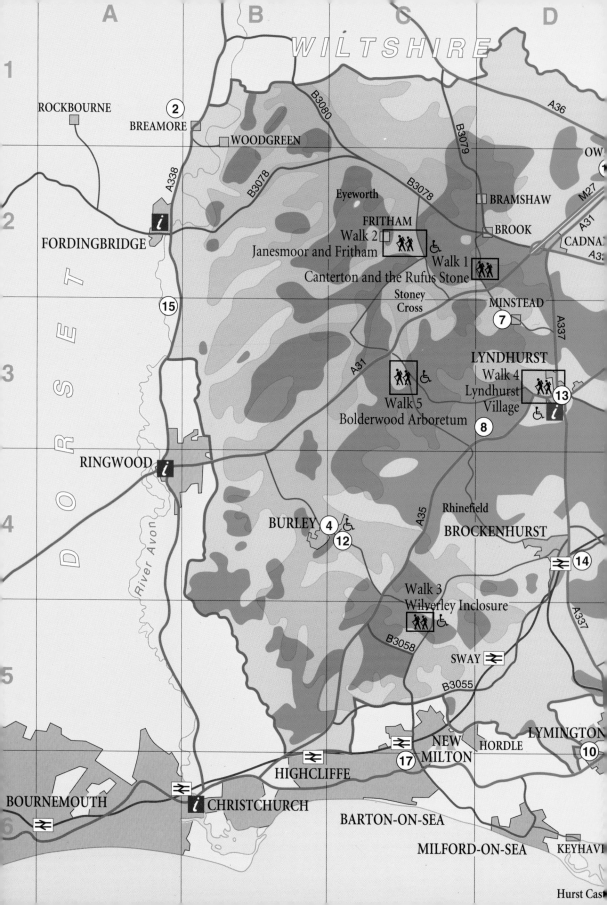

VISITING AND STAYING IN THE NEW FOREST

There is much for the visitor to see and enjoy along with a wealth of good quality accommodation to suit every pocket and taste.

New Forest Tourism is an association of tourism operators whose members are committed to providing the highest quality facilities and to ensuring that visitors enjoy the best possible stay in the district.

In partnership with District Council's Tourism Service, New Forest Tourism has developed the New Forest Encounter. In the company of people who have lived and worked there throughout their lives, the Encounter tells first hand the remarkable story of the New Forest's age old culture and natural heritage.

Around the edges of the New Forest are many interesting and exciting visitor attractions. All are members of New Forest Tourism. Further details and free colour guides on accommodation and places to visit can be obtained from Tourist Information Centres in the district (see page 45).

BELOW LEFT:
Camping has long been a favourite way to enjoy the forest.

BELOW RIGHT:
Visitors share the memories of a retired forest agister on a New Forest Encounter. A variety of different Encounters is available, each taking the visitor on an interesting journey of discovery through some of the most attractive and scenic parts of the forest.

The numbers cross-refer to the map on pages 22–23.

BEAULIEU, THE NATIONAL MOTOR MUSEUM   1
Tells the story of motoring from 1849 to the present. Also exhibition of monastic life in the atmospheric abbey ruins.

BREAMORE HOUSE AND COUNTRY-SIDE/CARRIAGE MUSEUMS   2
Elizabethan manor with a fine collection of art and furniture. Countryside Museum displays the history of agriculture and rural life.

BUCKLERS HARD MARITIME MUSEUM   3
18th-century village where ships of Nelson's fleet were once built. Museum with models, pictures, shipbuilder's drawings and relics.

BURLEY WAGONETTE RIDES, THE CROSS, BURLEY   4
Horse-drawn wagon rides through the forest and the attractive village of Burley.

ELING TIDE MILL   5
The only tidemill in western Europe producing wholewheat flour as it did centuries ago.

EXBURY GARDENS   6
200-acre woodland garden incorporating the world famous Rothschild collection of rhododendrons, azaleas, camellias and maples.

FURZEY GARDENS, MINSTEAD 7

8 acres of landscaped gardens, beautiful banks of azaleas, rhododendrons, heathers and many other interesting and rare shrubs.

HOLIDAYS HILL REPTILLIARY, LYNDHURST 8

Snakes, lizards and other reptiles and amphibians at close quarters .

LEPE COUNTRY PARK 9

Commands superb views across Solent. Parking, toilets, restaurant and children's play area.

LYMINGTON VINEYARD, PENNINGTON 10

Unguided walks, herb garden, slide show and free wine tasting. Open May to end of September.

LONGDOWN DAIRY FARM, ASHURST 11

A modern farm at work with all the fun of a children's farm. Dairy cattle, pigs, poultry. Video room, farm and gift shop. Picnic area.

NEW FOREST BUTTERFLY FARM, ASHURST 11

Free-flying fantasia of the world's most beautiful butterflies inside a tropical garden. Wagon rides, free adventure playground and picnic area, restaurant, gift shops.

NEW FOREST CIDER, BURLEY 12

Commoner's smallholding where cider is made the old-fashioned way. Taste and buy draught cider. Children's play area and farm animals.

NEW FOREST MUSEUM AND VISITOR CENTRE, LYNDHURST 13

The perfect place to start your exploration of the New Forest. AV show and exciting displays tell the story of the forest, its history, traditions, characters, legends and wildlife.

ABOVE:
The Rio Grande train ride is a popular attraction at Paultons Park, Ower. Kids' Kingdom has a giant slide, cableways and many other play activities.

RIGHT:
One of the many high-quality hotels in the forest.

BELOW:
The National Motor Museum at Beaulieu attracts thousands of visitors to its internationally renowned car collection. The museum is in the grounds of Beaulieu Abbey, now a picturesque ruin.

NEW FOREST WAGONS, BALMER LAWN ROAD, BROCKENHURST 14

Travel through car-free forest inclosures on wagons pulled by magnificent heavy horses.

NEW FOREST WATER PARK NORTH GORLEY, FORDINGBRIDGE 15

Family water ski, jet ski and aqua centre.

PAULTONS PARK, OWER 16

Exciting day out for all ages. Exotic birds and animals, extensive gardens, lake, watermill, Romany and Village Life Museums, Kids' Kingdom.

SAMMY MILLER MUSEUM, NEW MILTON 17

Large collection of classic racing and trial bikes.

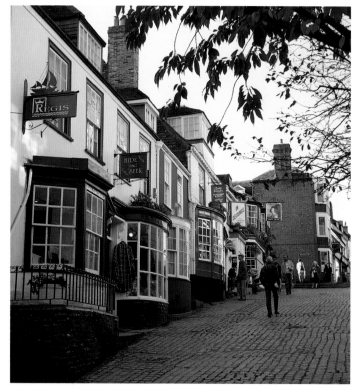

These are some of the many small historic towns and picturesque villages in and around the New Forest. The grid locations refer to the map on pages 22–23.

BARTON-ON-SEA   C6
Safe beach backed by low cliffs.

BEAULIEU   F4
Charming village on the Beaulieu River. Ruined 13th-century abbey and Palace House are in the grounds of the Beaulieu Estate.

BOLDRE   E5
Small village on Lymington River, with delightful 13th-century church. 'Spinners' has beautiful landscaped gardens open to the public.

BROCKENHURST   D4
The forest ponies and donkeys often visit the main street of Brockenhurst and graze on the village green. Some of the most popular forest walks are found close to the village. New Park, to the north, is the site of the annual New Forest Show.

BURLEY   B4
Attractive and well known village set in horse riding country, with several stables. Open heathland nearby provides good walking.

ABOVE:
The ancient port of Lymington has delightful cobbled streets with fine Georgian and Victorian cottages.

LEFT:
A visit to the New Forest Museum in Lyndhurst is a delightful way to gain an insight into the life of the forest.

RIGHT:
Sunset on the Lymington River. A pleasant half-hour crossing on the ferry from Lymington takes you over to the Isle of Wight.

LYNDHURST D3

In the heart of the New Forest surrounded by both heath and forest. Good selection of shops and cafés. New Forest Museum and Visitor Centre is open all year (see page 28).

MILFORD-ON-SEA D6

Peaceful resort town with easy access to the forest. Safe beach, mainly shingle. Spectacular views of Isle of Wight and the Needles.

NEW MILTON C5

Excellent shopping facilities and a good base to explore the south of the New Forest.

RINGWOOD A4

Market town and good touring centre for the forest and the Avon valley. Modern shops, historic inns and thatched cottages.

ROCKBOURNE A1

The main street of thatched cottages follows the course of a delightful stream. 13th-century village church and 15th-century manor house. 70-room Roman villa with mosaics and hypocaust.

FORDINGBRIDGE A2

Small historical town with medieval seven-arched bridge over the Avon. Early English parish church and fine Georgian houses.

FRITHAM C2

Small unspoilt village in the north of the forest with famous Royal Oak Inn (see page 14).

HORDLE D5

Quiet farming village. Two miles away is Hordle Cliff, a totally unspoilt stretch of coastline.

HYTHE F3

The old part of the town has Georgian and Victorian buildings and a long pier with a narrow gauge railway which takes passengers for the ferry across the water to Southampton.

KEYHAVEN D6

One of the few remaining 'villages' on Hampshire's coast. Keyhaven marshes form a bird sanctuary. Regular summer ferry service to Hurst Castle.

LYMINGTON D5

Lively yachting and sailing town. Georgian and Victorian cottages, houses and shops. The attractive High Street has a market every Saturday. Car ferry operates all year from Lymington to Yarmouth on the Isle of Wight.

ABOVE:
Fordingbridge, an ancient crossing place on the Avon.

BELOW:
If you are cycling or walking, the forest has many delightful pubs for a snack or meal and a well-earned drink. Details can be found in the New Forest 'Where to Eat and Drink' guide.

SWAY D5

Captain Marryatt, author of *Children of the New Forest*, based much of the book around the village of Sway.

WOODGREEN B1

On the north-west edge of the forest in the Avon valley, overlooked by Castle Hill. Village hall contains delightful murals which depict local life and people.

LYNDHURST – A VILLAGE WALK

The walk begins at the New Forest Museum and Visitor Centre, in Lyndhurst's main car park. Turn left into the busy High Street, walk up to the traffic lights just past the Fox and Hounds and cross over. Near the top is the Crown Hotel, which was once an important coaching house. On the small hill opposite stands the parish church, a prominent landmark visible for miles around.

Just behind the church is the grave of the original 'Alice in Wonderland' immortalized by Lewis Carroll. She is buried in the grave of the Hargreaves' family who lived locally. Further on in the walk you will pass opposite the gatehouse, all that now remains of their estate at Cuffnells. Just beyond the parish church is the Queen's House, an imposing

FAR LEFT:
Whitewashed thatched cottages face the green where cricket is played in the summer.

RIGHT:
The Queen's House, site of a royal hunting lodge since medieval times, now the home of the Forestry Commission who manage this royal forest which today covers 104 square miles of heath and woodland.

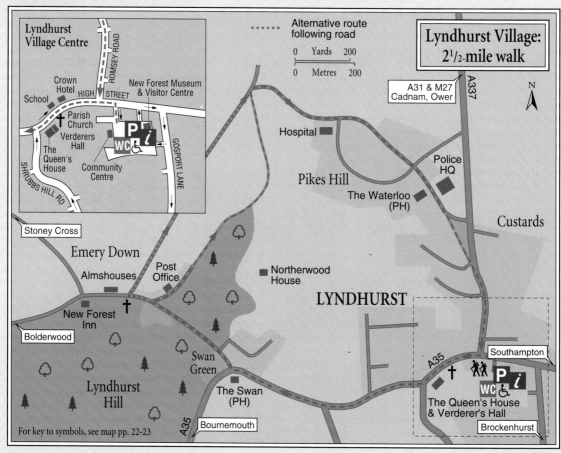

Lyndhurst Village Centre

Crown Hotel
School
HIGH STREET
ROMSEY ROAD
New Forest Museum & Visitor Centre
Parish Church
Verderers Hall
P
WC
i
The Queen's House
Community Centre
GOSPORT LANE
SHRUBBS HILL RD

Alternative route following road

0 Yards 200
0 Metres 200

Lyndhurst Village: 2½-mile walk

A31 & M27 Cadnam, Ower
A337
N

Hospital

Police HQ

Pikes Hill

The Waterloo (PH)

Custards

Stoney Cross

Emery Down

Almshouses

Post Office

Northerwood House

LYNDHURST

New Forest Inn

Bolderwood

Swan Green

Southampton

A35

The Queen's House & Verderer's Hall

WC
P
i

Lyndhurst Hill

The Swan (PH)

A35
Bournemouth

Brockenhurst

For key to symbols, see map pp. 22-23

brick building which stands on the site of the original Saxon manor house, claimed by William I before the time of the great Domesday survey in 1086. The building has remained in Crown ownership ever since and is now the main New Forest office of the Forestry Commission as well as home to the Court of Verderers. The ancient Verderer's Hall is on the left of the building, its Tudor foundations still visible.

Go straight on for 400 metres to Swan Green and turn right where attractive thatched cottages overlook the cricket pitch. Keep to the pavement beside the green and go over the cattle grid.

At the top of the hill is the neat little hamlet of Emery Down. Just over the brow of the hill, opposite an attractive forest 'lawn'

is Silver Street. Turn right here. You will pass the small post office and general store. Follow the street to the end, where it eventually becomes a well-defined bridlepath. Follow this between woodland and quiet pastures for several hundred metres. This is the gentle rural face of Lyndhurst which few people, other than its residents, ever see.

The track eventually joins a surfaced road at a small but sometimes busy junction. Turn sharp right and continue down the lane for 400 metres into the residential district which is known as Pikes Hill. There is no footpath here so look out for traffic as you walk. The lane swings right again opposite a small piece of grazed forest lawn close to what is thought to be the source of the Beaulieu River. This is marked by a well stone in a private garden nearby. The lane leads you past the Waterloo Arms, a popular forest pub. Do not cross the road, but go straight over the green ahead of you. The path eventually rejoins the main road and will lead you back to the High Street and the Museum and Visitor Centre.

ABOVE AND LEFT:
Lyndhurst's High Street has changed little in the last 100 years.

RIGHT:
The New Forest Museum and Visitor Centre is situated in the heart of the village and is open all year round. Also located in this building is the New Forest's main Tourist Information Centre.

WILDLIFE

Wildlife is found in abundance not just in the rare plants, birds and insects for which the forest is internationally important but in everyday encounters with the more common species.

In the forest, deer browse peacefully beneath the trees, eating the leaves and young shoots. Fallow deer are most common but red deer and sika deer, the two largest species in this country, can also be found while the small roe deer often slip quietly away before being noticed.

Britain's six native reptiles all live in the forest. Both the smooth snake and the sand lizard are now exceptionally rare in Britain, though the adder, our only venomous snake, is common in the forest. It is wary of humans and avoids people if it can.

ABOVE:
The wild gladiolus is an internationally rare plant carefully protected in the forest.

vibration of its tail feathers as the bird flies fast around its territory. The cuckoo calls from first light until late evening when it overlaps with the extraordinary twilight call of the nightjar. This bird arrives each May and nests on the ground in heather and bracken, feeding in the half light on abundant insect food. Many people hear its rhythmic mechanical 'churring' after dark, never realizing that a bird is responsible for this extraordinary sound.

The variety of habitats in the forest also attracts birds of prey. Buzzards, kestrels and sparrowhawks are common sights throughout the year. In summer the sickle-winged hobby, a fast moving falcon, hunts over the heath while in winter the stunning silver-grey-backed male hen harrier and brown 'ringtail' females sweep low to the ground over heather moorland and silent valley bottom as they search for prey.

Of the rich bird population England's only resident warbler, the tiny Dartford warbler, is a symbol of the great value of the open heaths. A rare bird nationally, it is abundant here, a small insect-feeder relying on well-managed heather and gorse for its well-being. In May and June the wet valleys ring out with the song of redshank, curlew and lapwing. The strange bleating sound of snipe can also be heard, a noise produced by the rapid

ABOVE:
The New Forest contains the largest expanse of lowland heath in north-west Europe.

ABOVE RIGHT:
Controlled burning of the heather by the Forestry Commission in the late winter ensures regeneration and fresh shoots for grazing animals.

During the summer months the heath is bursting with song from dawn to dusk. Skylarks, meadow pipits and the now rare woodlarks sing high above the ground. Even the smell of the forest becomes more potent at twilight as the moisture and scent of sweet gale (or bog myrtle) rises from the damp earth. The months of July and August bring the heather blossom, when beekeepers place hives on the open forest for the harvest of heather honey. The tiny silver-studded blue butterfly is common here because of the heather, along with hosts of nectar-feeding insects seeking the purple bloom.

In the wetter parts some quite rare plants still thrive like the insect-trapping sundew, the brilliant blue marsh gentian and the bog asphodel with its yellow-flowered spikes, known locally as 'brittle bones' because it was once thought to cause that condition in grazing animals. But the jewel in the botanical crown is the slender wild gladiolus, with its reddish-purple flowers, which grows nowhere else in Britain.

In this treasured part of England a richness of wildlife still remains to reward those who are prepared to look, to listen and be patient. The New Forest truly deserves its recognition as a nature reserve of international status.

LEFT:
The New Forest holds the largest population of the Dartford warbler in this country. This tiny bird is Britain's only resident species of warbler.

BELOW:
Many species of dragonfly breed in the forest; the common hawker is often seen.

LEFT:
The secretive nightjar builds its nest on the open heath. A summer visitor seldom seen by day, it is more often heard 'churring' after dark.

BELOW:
Ponies graze deep in the ancient pasture woodland.

W·A·L·K

Fallow deer provide the focus for this walk of just over 1½ miles (2.4 kilometres). The walk begins at the main car park by Bolderwood Green. Cross the road to the deer observation platform. In the field beyond, the deer are fed daily by Forestry Commission keepers throughout the year (except during the autumn when food is plentiful and mating takes place). This encourages some of them to stay in the area, although they are wild and will roam away if disturbed. A pair of binoculars is a real advantage as there is no predicting how close the deer will feed.

Return to the road and go left (north) for a short distance until you reach a grass ride on your left. Follow this for several hundred metres through stands of holly trees until you reach the main gravel road. Groups of old hollies, known throughout Britain as 'hollins', are known locally as 'holms' or 'hats'. Holly holms are found all over the New Forest on the better-drained valley sides. To ponies, cattle and deer they offer shelter and

ABOVE:
For most of the year a herd of fallow deer can be seen from the viewing platforms at Bolderwood.

BELOW:
The commoners' own cattle which are allowed to graze the forest.

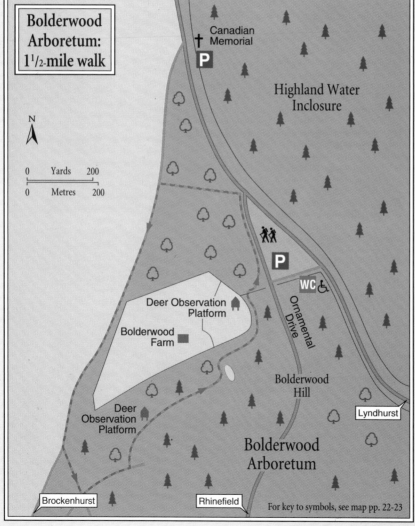

Bolderwood
Arboretum:
1½-mile walk

N

0 Yards 200
0 Metres 200

† Canadian Memorial
P

Highland Water Inclosure

P

WC ♿

Deer Observation Platform

Bolderwood Farm

Ornamental Drive

Deer Observation Platform

Bolderwood Hill

Lyndhurst

Bolderwood Arboretum

Brockenhurst

Rhinefield

For key to symbols, see map pp. 22-23

the berries offer a valuable source of food, especially the flocks of winter thrushes – redwings, fieldfares and blackbirds – flying in from the north.

Continue down the gravel road to your left for about 400 metres, entering the Bolderwood deer grounds. Here it is essential that all dogs are kept on leads. You will eventually enter the conifer plantation, a startlingly different habitat for forest wildlife – a secret sanctuary for deer and other large mammals which are always present but seldom seen. The walk continues along the ride to your left. At a second junction branch off to the left. This gravel track leads you through the fine tree collection known as the Bolderwood Arboretum. Sadly it suffered extensive storm damage during the gales of 1987 and 1990. It will be many years before restoration is complete. Towering douglas firs planted here in 1860 are now fully mature. Some, exceeding 45 metres, are the tallest examples in Britain. It is worth taking a track to the right of the pond to pass the Radnor Stone, part way up the hill amongst the trees. From the stone a short walk to the top of the hill takes you back to your starting point.

food, both bark and leaves being a favourite food – especially the new rubbery growth of young plants. Constant browsing accounts for the mushroom-shaped bushes and other curiously trimmed shrubs you will see around the forest. In winter, holly is cut to provide feed for the animals and also to supply city markets at Christmas. To wild birds

ABOVE:
Many different toadstools and mushrooms grow in the forest. The poisonous fly agaric is very common in the autumn.

BELOW LEFT:
Autumn colours bring many visitors. Dead wood is left on the forest floor as a home for insects and fungi.

BELOW:
The Radnor Stone was erected in memory of Lord Radnor, a Forestry Commissioner and subsequently a verderer.

ABOVE:
The adder's markings show well on this female. All three British species of snake can be seen at the Holidays Hill reptilliary off the A35 near Rhinefield.

BELOW:
The Forestry Commission reptilliary at Holidays Hill runs a breeding programme for rare reptiles which are released onto suitable sites. It is open daily during the summer months.

The New Forest is one of Britain's most important conservation areas, containing the country's largest remaining area of lowland heath which offers tremendous late-summer vistas of purple heather. The bogs and mires where forest streams start their gentle flow to the sea are some of our richest wildlife habitats, home to many rare plants and insects.

The forest's unique character and history is responsible for their survival. Marsh gentian or bog orchid can only survive because

the grazing of forest animals prevents them from being choked by more vigorous plants. The carnivorous sundews get their nourishment from eating insects and grow where there are few natural nutrients in the ground. Some insects have adapted their way of life to find a niche where they can survive and reproduce using the shelter of a hoof-print for their homes. Without the constant grazing of animals these precious areas would soon be lost.

Much of the New Forest has special protection under the 1981 Wildlife Act and English Nature, the government's conservation specialist, becomes involved in many management decisions. The New Forest keepers hold an ancient office which goes directly back to the time of William the Conqueror. Each keeper was responsible for a 'walk' and was answerable to the King for the control of pests and the management of the deer.

Today the forest is divided into 12 beats, each with its own resident keeper under two head keepers. Keepers are now employed by the Forestry Commission but in some ways their job remains the same as they still control

LEFT:
As part of their conservation work, New Forest keepers monitor the breeding success of sparrowhawks.

BELOW:
Sparrowhawk with young; these birds normally build their nests in conifer trees.

RIGHT:
A silver-washed fritillary feeding on bramble. This butterfly is a handsome and conspicuous inhabitant of New Forest oak woodlands. The forest has a rich butterfly population. Work is carried out to improve their habitats and ensure the right food plants are readily available.

pests and manage the deer. Each spring they count the number of deer on their beat and with their head keeper agree a shooting plan to keep a healthy balance between food supply and deer numbers. Today's keepers are also skilled in conservation. Living deep in the woods, they have a detailed knowledge of the wildlife. An important part of their job is to ensure that the needs of animals are recognized as the woodlands are managed.

Although their role has developed over 900 years the keepers' part in preserving the life of the forest is as important as ever.

RIGHT:
Wildlife monitoring is an important aspect of a keeper's work. Here a keeper takes careful note of the butterfly species present along a woodland ride in summer.

BELOW:
Leading Keeper Derek Thomson has spent many years studying the forest reptiles and was responsible for establishing the reptilliary at Holidays Hill.

FOREST IMAGES

RIGHT:
Ponies graze whilst golfers play on one of the three courses built on the forest by the Victorians.

BELOW:
Picnicking is a popular summer activity, but ponies should not be given titbits as they become a nuisance and will bite and kick for more food.

RIGHT:
Horse-riding is a popular forest activity. A code is published by the Forestry Commission to help riders protect forest wildlife and minimize erosion.

RIGHT:
Litter is unsightly and can be dangerous if eaten by ponies and cattle.

BELOW:
There are many villages with welcoming shops for visitors to explore. Burley is a popular forest village with a variety of shops and places to eat.

RIGHT:
The New Forest was created in 1079 as a royal hunting forest. The tradition continues to this day.

FAR LEFT:
Forests are valuable classrooms to teach children about the environment.

LEFT:
One of the well-equipped holiday centres in the forest, offering a wide variety of accommodation and facilities.

THE FUTURE OF THE FOREST

In 1863 the Victorian writer J.R.Wise* wrote 'The time will some day arrive when as England becomes more and more over-crowded – as each heath and common are swallowed up – the New Forest will be as much a necessity to the country as the parks are now to London'. But this unique area, having survived for the best part of a thousand years, is under threat as the pressures of modern living make more and more demands upon the countryside and the environment. Housing developments on the edge of the forest bring more people, road improvements nibble away at forest land and faster journeys make it easier for visitors to travel here. The threats of oil exploration and bigger power stations bring with them demands for pipelines and power lines across the forest landscape.

The New Forest is not a national park but in 1992 the government saw that it needed extra protection if it was to survive for future generations, deciding that it should have a special status similar to that of a national park, the New Forest Heritage Area. At the

*The New Forest, Its History and Scenery (1863)

RIGHT:
In recent years speeding traffic posed an increasing problem to the forest's animal population, with many ponies and cattle being killed or injured. Since 1992 a 40 mph speed limit has been in force across the whole forest bringing a dramatic drop in animal casualties.

moment the New Forest Committee, an informal group of official organizations under an independent chairman, co-ordinates management and planning. Soon this will be replaced by a statutory body.

The forest is the first area of countryside to have a blanket 40 mph speed limit. This

ABOVE:
By ancient tradition the ponies have right of way on forest roads. The car has to give way to grazing animals.

LEFT:
At busy times of the year forest roads become congested with traffic.

has reduced animal deaths on the road by a third and human injuries by a half. Many people suggest fencing off the roads but this would be to erode part of the charm and character of the forest.

As we have shown in this book, the continuance of the commoning tradition is essential to the well-being of the forest's unique and important plant and wildlife communities. But commoning too is under threat. The forest is an attractive area in which to live. Because good road and railway networks pass close by, many people move here but work elsewhere. This pushes up the price of land and houses, making it harder and harder for local families to buy holdings. To help them, a housing trust was founded in 1992 so that genuine commoners who put out stock can continue to live in the area thus carrying on the centuries-old tradition of the forest.

Each year many millions of people visit this wonderful place to share its peace and tranquillity. Here they are welcomed, for each visitor is an ally to the forest. By seeing, enjoying and understanding the qualities which make the forest so precious, each will play their part in its protection. It's true that there are some restrictions on what people can do, but nothing is done without good reason,

and people involved and working in the forest are only too happy to explain why. The addresses on page 45 of this book will lead you to further information. We are all stewards of the forest. To each of us, whether resident, forester, commoner or visitor, is entrusted the responsibility of ensuring that our children's children will inherit a place as precious to them as it is to us, the New Forest.

ABOVE:
Cycling on the roads and made-up gravelled tracks is a stimulating and increasingly popular way of seeing the forest.

RIGHT:
Walking in the forest is perhaps the most popular activity of all with many rewards in store for those prepared to explore the many forest tracks. Dogs should always be kept on leads in the inclosures to protect the deer. On the open forest dogs should be under close control to protect the wildlife, particularly ground-nesting birds.

THE NEW FOREST CODE

ROADS

Driving at 40mph or below on all unfenced forest roads greatly reduces the number of accidents involving ponies, cattle and deer, especially at night.

PARKING

Stopping on roadsides causes congestion and damage to verges. Please use one of the 150 forest car parks.

PONIES

Ponies are wild and should not be fed by visitors – this only encourages them to stray onto dangerous forest roads.
Ponies and donkeys can be very aggressive and young children are particularly at risk – keep a safe distance from ponies.

DOGS

Dogs are a serious problem in the forest.
Pets should be kept under control at all times because of disturbance to wildlife.
In the inclosures they must be kept on a lead.

ACCESS

You may walk on any footpath or track unless it says otherwise. By keeping to paths you greatly reduce the risk of disturbance to wildlife and their habitats.

CYCLING

Cycling is a good way to see the forest, but please stay on the public roads and made-up gravelled tracks.

FIRE

Fire is a great threat to all habitats and wildlife.
Regrettably, no picnic or camp fires are allowed but barbecue sites are provided by the Forestry Commission.

LITTER

Litter should always be taken home or placed in the animal-proof bins at car parks.

CAR PARK THEFT

Remember to lock your car and always take valuables with you – the quietest car parks often provide the easiest opportunities for thieves!